Answered Prayer

A Practical Look at Biblical Prayer

By Tim Gregory

ISBN 978-0-615-36479-7

Please visit our web site at
www.powerofprayernow.org

"If ye abide in me, and my words abide in you, ye shall ask what ye will, and it shall be done unto you."
John 15:7

INTRODUCTION

"My people are destroyed for lack of knowledge:
because thou hast rejected knowledge, I will also
reject thee, that thou shalt be no priest to me: seeing
thou hast forgotten the law of thy God, I will also
forget thy children."
Hosea 4:6

      The Lord told the children of Israel in the Book of Hosea that they were being destroyed because of a lack of knowledge. It is unfortunate but often times our prayer life can be the same way; destroyed because of a lack of knowledge.

      Often Christians have a false understanding of prayer. What many believe about prayer cannot be supported by biblical references. To have a true understanding of prayer we must examine what the Bible says about the subject; not adding or taking away from the scriptures.

      Throughout this book we will take a biblical look at prayer. We will examine in an easy to understand format exactly what the Bible has to say about prayer. The points given throughout this book will be backed up with references from the scriptures and also biblical examples.

Answered Prayer is written in a way that can benefit the mature Christian or the new believer. Both will find *Answered Prayer* to be a blessing, and a wealth of information on prayer from a biblical perspective.

Dedication

This book is dedicated to my wife, Julie. I cannot put into words what your love and support has meant to me throughout our marriage and this ministry the Lord has given us.

Table of Contents

Chapter 1

WHAT IS PRAYER?

"Give ear to my words, O LORD; consider my
meditation.
Listen to the voice of my cry, my King and my God;
for to You I will pray."
Psalms 5:1-2

Prayer defined is simply communication with God. Prayer is how we get in touch with God; it is our phone line to Heaven. If we want to make a call to a friend, we pick up the phone and dial the number. It is the same way when we want to talk to God; but instead of picking up the phone to call, we use prayer.

The great thing about prayer is that we are never too far away to make a call. I can carry my cell phone everywhere I go, but there are still times when my phone will not get reception. Prayer is different; no matter where I am when I pray, I am able to get hold of God through the phone line of Jesus Christ. As long as I am using Jesus Christ as my phone line, I can always get in touch with Heaven when I need to.

The Bible teaches us that if we will give God a call, He will show us great things. God will show us things that we could not understand on our own if we will just give Him a call. The problem arises when we don't call Him. God is always available and He wants us to call on Him, but it is up to us to pick up the phone and do it. If we will not call to God, we should not expect an answer. If we will call on God, whether in times of trial or peace, God will answer our calls.

In the Bible we read about a man named David. David became famous throughout the land when he killed the giant named Goliath.[i] David would eventually become king, but at the time of this story he was in hiding. He and the many people who followed him had taken refuge in a nearby country because king Saul of Israel sought to kill David.

One day David and his men returned home to find that the village they were living in had been invaded while they were gone; their wives, children, and livestock had all been taken. What horror these men must have felt to return home and find their families and all they owned gone!

David and his men were understandably in great distress. The Bible tells us they all wept terribly, and they continued to weep until they were exhausted and had no more strength. I can only imagine how helpless they must have felt not knowing where their wives and children were, or if they were even alive.

The men were greatly grieved, but grief quickly turned to anger. The men that followed David began to contemplate stoning their leader. Things had just gone from bad to worse for David. He could have just sat there and suckled in his misery, but instead he made a choice to call on the Lord. David put a call in to the only One who could help him. God was able to reveal to David that he would get back all that was taken if he would go after those who had raided their village. David and his men did as God told them and got back all that was taken; not even one person that had been taken was lost.[ii]

David was able to turn a hopeless situation around because he called on the Lord. God is never out of reach no matter how bad things may look. All we have to do is pick up the prayer line and make a call to the Lord. God is able to turn everything around!

PRAYER IS
WHAT MAKES ALL THINGS POSSIBLE

Prayer is the instrument that can turn everything around. We find that when we pray, the things that were seemingly impossible become possible. The Bible tells us, *"For with God nothing shall be impossible."*[iii]

When we go to God in prayer, we find He is able to do more than we could even ask. God's power is not limited. When we make a call to God, we are calling on the Creator of the Universe. There is absolutely nothing that is too hard for God.

David called on God, and God was able to turn a hopeless situation into a victorious one. David and his men were able not only to retake all that belonged to them, they also plundered the possessions of those who took from them. God was able to do exceedingly abundantly above all David and his men could ask or think.[iv]

Perhaps you are currently facing a situation that seems hopeless: the doctor has informed you that your cancer is spreading; your child is sick and the doctors have been unable to help. Regardless of what you may be going through, God can turn it around; but it all starts with you making a phone call to Heaven. When we call on the Lord, the impossible becomes possible. The praying man or woman of God who walks by faith can accomplish anything through Christ.[v]

PRAYER IS WHAT
UNLEASHES THE POWER OF HEAVEN

I have heard many people say they don't believe they need to pray for themselves because God already knows what they need. It is true; God knows the desire of your heart before you ever ask. He knows exactly what you need, but you still must ask. Many times we don't receive from God simply because we do not ask of Him. We cannot expect God to meet our needs if we do not ask Him. *"You desire, and do not have. You murder, and are jealous, and cannot obtain. You fight and war, **yet*** *you have not because you ask not.*[vi]   What a terrible thought!   We may miss out on God's provision for us simply because we will not ask.

Just as we wish to help our own children—to provide for their needs, and to make sure no harm comes to them—God, our Father in Heaven, wants to do the same for His children here on earth. God wants to provide for us; He wants to come to our aid when we are in distress, but we must call Him.

When we go to God in prayer, we release the power of Heaven into our situation. The Bible tells us that after Jesus was baptized He stood and prayed and Heaven was opened.[vii] We must keep in mind that God's will is not automatically done here on earth; that is why Jesus taught us to pray for it.[viii] God's will may be to deliver you from the situation you are going through right now; but if you do not ask Him, you may not receive His help.

In the Bible we read of Samson. Samson was the real superman. He had incredible strength that was unmatched. On his own, no man could stand against him or dare to challenge him. He was a man among men. One day, Samson's enemies came against him; there were a thousand of them. Even though there were a thousand men, they were still no match for Samson. The Spirit of the Lord came upon Samson, and he took the jawbone of a donkey that was lying nearby and used it to kill all one thousand men.

What an incredible victory God had brought him! Samson was understandably worn out and thirsty after the fight, so thirsty he though he was going to die. Surely God knew he was thirsty, but still there was no water provided for him to drink. God had already done so much for Samson by bringing him such a great victory; dare he ask for anything else? Samson did ask, and he received. Samson had a need and he called on the Lord. There was no water in sight, so Samson's request must have seemed impossible. How incredible for Samson, we have a God who is in the business of making the impossible possible. To quench Samson's thirst, God made water come out of the jawbone he had used in the fight.[ix] Nothing is impossible for God!

If Samson had not asked, he would have never received. God knew Samson had a need, and he wanted to meet that need; but Samson had to ask first. When he called on the Lord, the power of Heaven was unleashed; and God's will was accomplished in Samson's life.

If you have a request, don't hesitate to call on the Lord. If we will go to the Lord in prayer, the power of Heaven will be released into our lives; and the will of God will be accomplished in our lives here on earth. If we want to receive from our Father in Heaven, we must ask.

[1] 1 Samuel 17:48-50
[2] 1 Samuel 30:6
[3] Luke 1:37
[4] Ephesians 3:20
[5] Philippians 4:19
[6] James 4:2
[7] Luke 3:21
[8] Matthew 6:10
[9] Judges 15:18-19

Chapter 2

THE POTTED PLANT EFFECT

*"If you abide in Me, and My words abide in you,
you will ask what you desire, and it shall be done
for you."*
John 15:7

Jesus said we may ask for what we desire and it will be done for us. Wow! What a promise; ask what you want and it will happen. How easy it would be to take this out of context and try to use God as some sort of genie that pops out of a magical lamp to grant us anything we wish for. Yet, Jesus does say to ask and it will be given. Jesus said for us to be able to receive whatever we ask, we must first live in Him; and His words must live in us. If we are living in Christ and His words are living in us, we may ask anything we want and it will be done for us.

In these words that Christ has spoken, we have a picture of a potted plant. A potted plant starts with the pot. If there is no pot, there is nothing to put the soil and the seed into. If you have a pot, you then must have good soil. If the soil is no good, the seed will not be able to take root and grow. Then we must have a seed or no plant will grow; and if no plant grows, obviously there will be no fruit. The seed will also need adequate water and sunlight to develop to its full potential.

If we look at this analogy in the light of the words of Christ, He is the pot; nothing will grow outside of Him, and anything that is going to produce fruit must be in Him. We are the soil that goes into the pot. If the soil of our hearts is too hard, the seed will not be able to take root and grow properly. The seed is the Word of God. God's Word is to be planted in our hearts. The water and sunlight that cause the seed to grow is faith. When faith is applied to God's Word that is planted in the good ground of our hearts, the Word will grow and produce fruit; it is at this point that we may ask anything we desire and it will be done.

Let us now take a closer look at the pot of Christ, the soil of our hearts, the seed of God's Word, and the nourishment to that Word which is faith that causes it to grow and produce fruit.

Chapter 3

THE POT: ABIDING IN CHRIST

"You were taught, with regard to your former way of life, to put off your old self, which is being corrupted by its deceitful desires; to be made new in the attitude of your minds; and to put on the new self, created to be like God in true righteousness and holiness."
Ephesians 4:22-24 (NIV)

For my prayer life to be effective, I must abide in Christ. I must live in Christ if I wish to see fruit produced when I pray. It is only through Jesus Christ that all things are possible; so if I expect to be able to ask of God and receive, I must go through Jesus— meaning I am abiding in Christ. Jesus Christ is the pot that holds our lives together, the pot we fit into if we are to have a fruitful prayer life.

When I am abiding in Christ, I am dead to the person I once was. I am crucified with Christ; the body of sin that I once lived in is gone. When Jesus died on the cross, He paid the penalty for the sins of all mankind. When I accept the sacrifice He made on the cross and choose to make Him the Lord of my life, I come to abide in Him. The sinful person I once was I consider dead, crucified with Jesus Christ.

When I am dead to the person I once was, the Bible teaches me that I am born again. When I am born again, I do not go back into my mother's womb; but I receive the Spirit of God that brings life to my spirit that was once dead. I look the same on the outside, but it is the inside that has been changed. The first time we are born, it is of flesh and blood; but the second time it is a spiritual rebirth.[1]   To abide in Christ means to be born again. You cannot abide in Christ if you are not born again.

When I abide in Christ, being born again, I become a new person. When I abide in Christ, I see things differently. Because I am a new person viewing the world through new eyes, I no longer live by my own strength but by the power of God living in me. Once I did whatever I wanted, living by a false sense of self-righteousness; but now I depend and rely on His righteousness. When I abide in Christ as a new person with a new life, I am depending on Jesus Christ for the strength to live a life pleasing to God.

The apostle Paul once persecuted the early church. He set out to destroy the church any way he could. When Paul met up with Jesus Christ, the man he once was died; and he was born again. Paul became a new person when he made a decision to abide in Christ, accepting Jesus as the Lord of his life. Paul said that he recognized himself as being crucified with Christ, dead to his old ways. The life he now lived was according to the will of God. Paul went from being a destroyer of the church to being a builder. He was a new creation abiding in Christ. Paul was not a perfect man; but he was a new man abiding in Christ, depending on the power of God living inside him, and not his own strength.

In Paul's letter to the Galatian church he said, *"I am crucified with Christ: nevertheless I live; yet not I, but Christ liveth in me: and the life which I now live in the flesh I live by the faith of the Son of God, who loved me, and gave himself for me."* [2] Abiding in Jesus means I am living in Him, depending on Him at all times; He is my focus continually. When I am in Christ, I no longer look on my own accomplishments but on those of Christ. I depend on His righteousness and His finished work on the cross. When I abide in Christ, "self" is taken out of the picture; and it is truly all about Jesus and what He has done.

When we are abiding in Christ, we become children of God. The Bible teaches us that all who accept Christ become children of God.[3] Abiding in Christ does not mean I will never make mistakes; but it does mean I am walking a new path, seeing things in a new way, and depending on the power of the Holy Spirit inside me that I have received through Jesus Christ.

When God's children are abiding in Christ, all things are possible to them; they may do as Jesus said and ask whatever they will, and it will be done so that their Father in heaven may be glorified.

[1] John 3:3-6
[2] Galatians 2:20
[3] John 1:12

Chapter 4

THE SOIL

"A good man out of the good treasure of the heart bringeth forth good things: and an evil man out of the evil treasure bringeth forth evil things."
Matthew 12:35

The pot we must abide in is Jesus Christ. We are the soil that goes into the pot. No matter what is planted, if the soil is not good, the seed will not grow properly. The seed may not sprout, or it may even grow into a plant but not produce fruit. The seed must be able to take root, so it can draw from the soil the nutrients that it needs to grow. Many roots will penetrate the soil and begin to grow only to find that some weeds were never removed and are mixed in the dirt. Because the weeds and the good plant both fight for nutrients from the soil, neither one grows as it should. For a seedling to take root and grow, the soil must be clean and loose; this is good fruit-producing soil.

Man's heart is the soil that the Word of God is planted in. The soil must be good for the Word of God to grow and produce fruit in our prayer lives. When the soil is good, our prayers are able to

21

produce fruitful treasures for the Kingdom of God. When the soil is good and our prayers produce fruit, God is glorified. Jesus said, *"By this My Father is glorified, that you bear much fruit; so you will be My disciples."* [1] When the Word of God is growing in our hearts, our prayers will be answered; and fruit that will bring glory to the Kingdom of God will be produced from those prayers.

Jesus tells a story of a man who went out to sow some seed. As he threw the seeds out, some of them fell on the roadside. The ground there was hard and the seed could not penetrate it, so it lay on top of the ground and the birds came and ate it up. Some of the other seed that was thrown out fell on rocky ground. There wasn't much soil there and it wasn't very deep. The seeds sprang up quickly; but because there wasn't much soil, they were not able to take root. The sun scorched them and they died. Other seed fell on ground where thorns had been left. The seeds were able to take root there and grow, but so were the thorns. The thorns grew up beside the seed and choked the plants out, keeping them from producing fruit. Still, there were some seeds that fell on good ground where the thorns had been cleaned out. These plants produced much fruit. [2]

Each of the four kinds of soil represents the different hearts that are found in men. We will now look at each of these hearts.

THE ROAD SIDE

The soil of the heart that is represented by the roadside is a hard-beaten path that has never been ploughed up. The heart is hard, and the Word of God will not sink into it. The soil of this heart has been tightly packed down from constant skepticism, bitterness, and other circumstances of life. When the person attempts to pray, no fruit is produced because this heart will not receive the Word of God. This heart continues to harden, not allowing the mercy of God to soften it. Because the Word of God is not allowed to penetrate the heart, the evil one comes quickly and steals it away.

We read in the Bible of a king named Agrippa. When the apostle Paul was being held captive waiting to be sent before Caesar, King Agrippa came along and was interested to hear what Paul had to say. Agrippa knew that Paul had a disagreement with some of the Jews about a religious topic; but he was still unsure, having only heard about it second hand. When Paul came before him, he began to tell Agrippa about his encounter with Jesus Christ and how he was converted. Paul spoke to Agrippa concerning what the prophets had written about Jesus. Agrippa was surely very moved; he even told Paul that he had almost convinced him to become a Christian.[3] Agrippa could not receive the Word of God because his heart was hardened by skepticism. There are those today who hear God's Word but are very critical of it. They are not willing to accept it as the only truth; their hearts are hard. They have never had the hard ground of their hearts broken up, nor do they wish to. Because they are always critical and in doubt of God's Word, it has never penetrated their hearts; and the evil one has come and stolen it away. When they decide to give prayer a try, it is unfruitful because God's Word is not in their hearts.

ROCKY GROUND

This is the heart that hears God's Word and gladly receives it. The seed of God's Word begins to grow; but there is not much soil, so it cannot take root. This is the heart that gets excited when it hears the Word of God. It is evident that this person has been moved by the Word; but because the soil was not right, the Word quickly dies out. Persecution arises in the individual's life, and he is quickly offended; the Word withers away and dies. It was never able to take root and flourish. The prayer life of this individual will not produce fruit for the Kingdom of God.

The heart that will not allow the Word of God to penetrate it and take root will not produce fruit for the Kingdom of God. If we will not give place to God's Word when He gives it to us, our prayer will not be in line with the Word of God, making it ineffective. We must receive God's Word when it is given. Then our prayers will line up with the Word and be received and answered by the Lord when we call. Otherwise, our prayers will go unanswered.

The Lord said in the book of Zechariah concerning Israel, *"And they made their hearts like the hardest stone, so that they might not give ear to the law and the words which the Lord of armies had said by the earlier prophets: and there came great wrath from the Lord of armies. And it came about that **as they would not give ear to his voice, so I would not give ear to their voice, says the Lord of armies***.*"[4] This describes the ineffectiveness of the prayer lives of those today who will not allow God's Word to penetrate their hearts.

The heart that is depicted as rocky ground by Jesus is the heart of those who believe God's Word when they hear it, and even sing His praises, but soon forget His Word and works and do their own thing. A person whose heart is made of "rocky ground" will not have an effective prayer life; fruit will not be produced.

SOIL WHERE THORNS GROW

Jesus tells of a third kind of soil in His story. In this soil the seed is able to grow and take root, but there are also thorns growing up with the seed. The ground has been plowed and broken up, but it has not been maintained. Thorns have made their way into the soil and are now growing by the good seed. These thorns compete for the nutrients in the soil, the rain that waters the ground, and the sun that shines on them. The good seed is in competition with the thorns, both of them fighting to grow and flourish. Neither is able to grow to their fullest potential because they are forced to share the nutrients provided by the soil, both always lacking what is needed to truly flourish.

The soil of our hearts must be maintained. When the seed of God's Word is planted into a good heart, Satan is not far behind. The enemy comes to plant seeds of fear, worry, and doubt. These seeds planted by the enemy will grow up beside the Word of God if the soil of our hearts is not continually maintained. Any garden that is planted must be maintained and cared for; if it is not, weeds and thorns will eventually overtake it. The garden of the heart is no different. God plants good seed, and Satan plants thorns of destruction. The soil of our hearts must be constantly cared for and watched over if the Word of God is going to grow and produce fruit.

When the soil of our hearts is littered with doubts and fears planted by the enemy, our prayer lives will not produce the fruit they should. God's Word may be living in our hearts, but so are fear and doubt. The thorns of fear, worry, and doubt must be removed so that God's Word can grow and produce fruit. Jesus said, *"No man can serve two masters: for either he will hate the one, and love the other; or else he will hold to the one, and despise the other. Ye cannot serve God and mammon. Therefore I say unto you, Take no thought for your life, what ye shall eat, or what ye shall drink; nor yet for your body, what ye shall put on. Is not the life more than meat, and the body than raiment?"* [5]

If our hearts are constantly being pulled in two different directions, our prayer lives will not produce fruit for no man can serve two masters. No man can be productive for two lords. We must heed the words of our Savior and cast the fear and worry from our hearts. When we do this the Word of God will grow, and our prayer lives will produce fruit.

In the Bible we read of a king of Judah named Amaziah. The Bible tells us that Amaziah followed God, but not with all of his heart. Amaziah worshiped the Lord but he also worshiped false gods of the people he had conquered. Amaziah's heart was divided; God had part of it, but so did the enemy. [6] Amaziah's kingdom never flourished like it could have because his heart was divided between two masters. Two different seeds were planted in his heart, and both struggled for dominance. Amaziah was not able to serve two masters and chose the wrong one, turning from God. If we do not tend to the soil of our hearts, the enemy will sow seed in it; and we will find ourselves struggling between two masters. Our prayer lives may at times produce some minimal fruit, but they will never produce fruit for the Kingdom of God that they could if they were not divided.

GOOD GROUND

The last type of soil that Jesus speaks of is called "good ground." This soil is where the earth is deep, and the ground has been thoroughly plowed. The thorns and weeds have been removed, and the soil is tended to on a regular basis. The soil is rich in nutrients, and the planted seed will yield much fruit.

This soil represents the heart that is ready to receive God's Word. These people hear the Word of God, receiving it gladly and retaining it. Regardless of the circumstances that arise in their lives, they hold onto God's Word. They continue to study God's written Word, walking and talking daily with Jesus Christ their Lord and Savior. They become mature Christians, growing in God's Word. The Word of God grows in their hearts because it is continually cultivated through daily Bible reading and prayer time. They pray according to the Word of God; and their prayers produce much fruit, bringing glory to the Kingdom of God.

The Lord said, *"A new heart also will I give you, and a new spirit will I put within you: and I will take away the stony heart out of your flesh, and I will give you an heart of flesh."*[7] A heart that is "good ground" is a new heart, one created by the Lord. This heart is free of the worries and cares of this world; it has released the things of old and embraced the things of God. The owner of this heart has allowed God to enter it and transform it. This heart of "good ground" is now able to view things from an eternal perspective, to walk by faith and not by sight. This heart relies on the Word of God; it is not divided between two views. It follows God all the way. The soil of this heart, which is labeled "good ground" by the Lord, will produce much fruit in its prayer life. When this heart calls on the Lord, He will hear and be moved to action for the prayer and request of this heart are guided by God's own Word. This ground will not only produce much fruit in its prayer life; but in doing so, it will bring glory to God.

The Bible tells us of a time after God had brought the people of Israel out of Egypt and was getting ready to bring them into a land flowing with milk and honey—a land that God Himself had promised to their fathers. Moses sent twelve spies to check out the land. The spies returned saying that it truly was a land flowing with milk and honey, but that it was a land occupied by giants. All but two of the spies felt that it was impossible for them to overtake the giants and claim the land as their own. All the spies knew the promise God had made, but only two of them believed it. The negative report the ten spies brought back caused the hearts of all the people to fall victim to fear and miss out on what God had promised; their hearts were not "good ground." But the hearts of two men, Joshua and Caleb, were hearts where the soil was right to produce fruit. Joshua and Caleb heard the Word of God and received it as truth; they held to it regardless of what they saw.[8] These two men walked by faith and not by sight. They believed God and trusted Him, and because of this they were the only adults out of a whole nation to receive what God had promised them. They were able to receive the promise because the Word of God grew in their hearts without thorns or weeds; their hearts were "good ground."

MAKING AND KEEPING GOOD GROUND

The question must now be asked, "What kind of soil is my heart made of?" Is my heart "good ground," or is it filled with thorns choking out the Word of God? Is my heart so hard that God's Word just lays on top unable to penetrate? Is my prayer life producing fruit, so that God is glorified? The good news is that if your prayer life is not producing fruit, it does not have to stay that way. The soil of our hearts can be changed.

If the soil of our hearts is not right to produce fruit, it can be changed; but you must be willing for it to change. God desires for our prayer lives to produce fruit, for when they do He is glorified. The seed of God's Word must be able to grow in our hearts for fruit to be produced when we call on Him in prayer. The hard ground must be broken up so that God's Word can penetrate it. The Bible says, *"For thus saith* *the LORD to the men of Judah and Jerusalem, **Break up your fallow ground,** and **sow not among thorns.**"*[9]

To make the soil of our hearts ready to receive God's Word it must be broken up. The ground has to be plowed. If the soil remains as it is, God's Word will not be able to penetrate and grow; and our prayer lives will not produce fruit. So our questions must be, "How do I plough the ground of my heart?" And "How do I get my heart ready to receive the seed of God's Word?" The Lord said, *"And Ephraim is a trained cow, taking pleasure in crushing the grain; but I have put a yoke on her fair neck; I will put a horseman on the back of Ephraim; **Judah will be working the plough,** Jacob will be turning up the earth. Put in the seed of righteousness, get in your grain in mercy, let your unploughed earth be turned up: for it is time to make search for the Lord, till he comes and sends righteousness on you like rain."*[10]

The word "Judah" literally means praise. When God says, *"Judah will be working the plough,"* He is literally saying, *"Praise will be working the plough."* To break up the hard ground of our hearts, we must praise God. When we praise God, the ground of our hearts is being broken up so that it will be ready and able to receive the seed of God's Word.

Praise, simply put, is a physical and verbal expression of our attitude toward God. Praise is an acknowledgement of God's worth, glory, and majesty. Praise is occupied with who God is and what He has done. Praise begins with a mind set upon God, but

31

those thoughts must be put into action to qualify as praise.

Praise can be direct or indirect. When I praise God directly, I am expressing to Him my gratitude for all He has done in my life. When I praise God indirectly, I am expressing my gratitude to someone else for all the Lord has done for me. When I tell others of God's goodness and mercy, I am indirectly praising him.

Praise is a function of the will—not the emotions. We must make a choice to praise God whether we feel like it or not, for it is praise that will prepare our hearts to receive God's Word. Remember it is easier to act your way into a feeling, than to feel your way into an action. Praise God regardless of how you feel; your emotions will eventually follow your actions. We must plow up the ground of our hearts so that it will always be ready and able to receive the seed of God's Word.

Beware of thorns sprouting up in your "good ground" once you have plowed it up. When the cares and worries of this life find their way into your heart, they choke out God's Word. To have a fruitful prayer life our hearts must remain fertile, ready and able to receive God's Word. We must continue to offer up to God the sacrifice of praise. In doing so we will keep the ground of our hearts plowed and free from the cares and worries of this world. Our hearts will be "good ground" where God's Word can grow and flourish; and our prayers will be productive, producing much fruit so that God will be glorified.

[1] John 15:8
[2] Matthew 13:3-8
[3] Acts 26:28
[4] Zechariah 7:12-13 (B.B.E.)
[5] Matthew 6 27-28
[6] 2 Chronicles 25:2
[7] Ezekiel 36:26
[8] Numbers chapter 13 & 14
[9] Jeremiah 4:3
[10] Hosea 10: 11-12

Chapter Five

THE SEED OF GOD'S WORD

"And this is the confidence that we have in him, that, if we ask any thing according to his will, he heareth us: And if we know that he hear us, whatsoever we ask, we know that we have the petitions that we desired of him."
1 John 5:14-15

For our prayers to be effective we must abide in the "Pot" of Jesus Christ. The "soil" of our hearts must be "good soil," ready to receive the seed. The "seed" which is God's Word must be planted in the "good soil" of our hearts. We must understand that the Word of God is the will of God; this is the seed that must be planted in our hearts. If our prayer lives are going to produce fruit, the Word of God must abide— that is actively live—in our hearts.

If our prayers are going to be answered, they must fall in line with the will of God. We will not know God's will unless the seed of His Word is growing in our hearts. When the seed of God's Word is growing in our hearts, we know God's will and are able to pray accordingly. God's will is revealed in His written Word and in His spoken Word. God speaks to our hearts by His Holy Spirit revealing His specific will to us. When the seed of God's Word—which is equal to His will—is abiding in our hearts, we will ask according to it and our prayers will be answered. This is the assurance we have from God himself.

GOD'S WRITTEN WORD

God's will is revealed to us in the Bible. God's written Word is never changing; since it was God's will two thousand years ago for us to pray for our enemies, it still is. Jesus said heaven and earth would pass away but His words would remain.[1] The Word of God is never changing!

When we receive the written Word of God into our hearts and it grows and flourishes there, our prayer lives will be prosperous. God told Joshua, *"This book of the law shall not depart out of thy mouth; but thou shalt meditate therein day and night, that thou mayest observe to do according to all that is written therein: for then thou shalt make thy way prosperous, and then thou shalt have good success."*[2]

We must know the Word of God in order to ask according to it. We must make a habit of reading our Bibles daily, so that the seed of God's Word may be planted in our hearts. God reveals much of what we are to pray for in His written Word. We are to pray for those who are in authority over us. This includes those who have authority over us in government and on the job. It also includes those who are in positions of spiritual authority such as your pastor. We are to pray for the lost—those who do not know Jesus as their Savior—for the Bible tells us it is God's will that all should be saved.[3] We are to pray for ourselves to become more like Jesus every day.[4] We must know the Bible so we can pray as God would have us pray. It is God's Word that brings forth fruit; so if we pray according to that Word, our prayers will be fruitful. When the seed of God's written Word is actively living in our hearts and directing our prayers so that we ask according to God's will, fruit will be produced; and God will be glorified because of it.

only seed produces fruit
no seed, no fruit

GOD'S SPOKEN WORD

There are times when God speaks directly to our hearts concerning His will. If the soil of our hearts is "good ground," we will be able to receive the seed of God's spoken Word when He gives it to us. For every situation we encounter, God has a specific will concerning that situation, something He wants to happen. Jesus teaches us that we are to pray for God's will to be done on earth just as it is in heaven.[5] We must understand that God's will is always done in heaven; but because of sin that is in the world, God's will is not always done on earth. When God speaks to our hearts revealing His will, we are able to pray accordingly.

When we pray according to God's will, the power of Heaven is released into whatever situation we have encountered. When the power of Heaven is

Pray His will to release Heaven

37

released upon this earth, God's will is going to be accomplished on this earth. There is incredible power released when we pray according to the seed of God's Word.

We read of Israel in the days of king Ahab when God closed the sky and allowed no rain to fall. For three years Israel suffered severe drought. The Word of the Lord came to the prophet Elijah saying that God would make the rain to fall again. Elijah knew it was God's will for it to rain for God had told him. There was no doubt about God's will, yet Elijah still had to pray for it to be done. The Bible tells us that Elijah went up to the top of Mount Carmel, bowed down, and put his face between his knees. Elijah knew God's will, but he still had to pray for it to be done on earth.

As we read the story, we find that after he prayed, Elijah sent his servant to look and see if rain was coming. The servant came back and reported that he saw no signs of rain. Elijah sent him back seven times before the servant came with a report that he saw signs of rain. Elijah did not give up on the will of God for it to rain upon the earth, even though it did not happen right away. When God speaks to our hearts concerning His will for our lives, we must pray accordingly, being persistent. Just because our prayers don't come to pass right away does not mean that we missed God. We must be persistent just as Elijah was concerning the will of God. When we pray according to God's Word for our lives and are persistent, it will come to pass; the windows of heaven will open and the power of heaven will rain down upon us.

THE CHILDREN
OF GOD DO THE WILL OF GOD

It is not always easy to understand God and His will. We know that God sees a picture that we can't. We know God's thoughts and His ways are higher than ours. Even though we may not always understand God's will, as His children, we are to follow His will. When we go to God in prayer and He says "No" we must accept that answer. We may never understand why God would say no to certain requests we make; but as children in His Kingdom, we do know that He loves us and has our best interest at heart.

"For as many as are led by the Spirit of God, these are sons of God."[6] We are God's children and it is through the Holy Spirit of God that we receive His Word. When the Spirit speaks to us, we are to follow. We must follow God's Word in life and in our prayer lives. When God says "No" it is no. As His children, we must accept His will.

We read in the Bible, in the Book of Jeremiah, of a time after the destruction of Jerusalem. At this time those who were not killed or taken captive by the Babylonians came to seek the Lord's will for their lives. They came to the prophet Jeremiah and asked him to inquire of the Lord what they should do. The people declared they would do whatever God said.

39

God replied and told the people to stay in their land and He would give them favor.[7] This was not the answer the people wanted; the people wanted to leave and go to Egypt. They came seeking the Lord's will, but really they only wanted God to agree with them. Even though they were God's chosen people and had seen His mighty work, they refused to follow His Word.

Many times today we are the same way when it comes to accepting God's will. We may not always understand God or even agree with Him; but we are His children, with His Spirit living inside us, and we are to do and accept His will. Ask God what you will. When he says "Yes" know that it will happen; but when God says "No" accept His answer as a child of God who is being led by the Spirit of God. God's Word is God's will; and for our prayers to be answered, they must fall in line with it.

1 Matthew 24:35
2 Joshua 1:8
3 2 Peter 3:9
4 Romans 8:29
5 Matthew 6:10
6 Romans 8:14
7 Jeremiah 42

Chapter Six

MOUNTAIN MOVING FAITH

"Jesus answered and said unto them, Verily I say unto you, If ye have faith, and doubt not, ye shall not only do this which is done to the fig tree, but also if ye shall say unto this mountain, Be thou removed, and be thou cast into the sea; it shall be done."
Matthew 21:21

When we pray, we can think of it as simply making a phone call to God. When we place our call there is only one line we can use, which is Jesus. Jesus is the only phone line that can connect us to Heaven and the Father. If prayer is a phone call to God, and Jesus is the phone line connecting us, faith would be the electricity in the line. We must have faith when calling the Lord. If we do not have faith in our prayers when we call on the Lord, our prayers will be ineffective.

The Bible says, *"Now faith is the substance of things hoped for, the evidence of things not seen."*[1] Faith starts as a hope that calls out to God. As this hope grows, God's Spirit testifies to our spirit that we may have the desire of our heart that falls in line with

His Word. At this point our hope is turned to faith. Faith is born of hope that prays until an answer comes.

The Bible tells us of a particular account when Jesus came to a certain city. A man full of leprosy, seeing Jesus, fell on his face before Him. The man with leprosy asked Jesus if He would make him clean. He knew Jesus was able to heal him if He were willing. The Bible says that Jesus put forth His hand, touching the man with leprosy and telling him that "Yes" it was His will for him to be clean. The Bible says that the leprosy immediately departed from him.[2]

The man with leprosy had a hope that Jesus would heal him. He had no doubt in the ability of Jesus to heal him. The man only hoped to hear Jesus say "Yes" to his request. The man's hope was turned to faith when Jesus said yes. Faith that heals comes only from Jesus. It is not our hope that moves mountains, but the "Yes" that comes from Jesus Christ. *Interesting*

JESUS IS OUR SUPPLIER OF FAITH

Jesus is the one who gives us the faith to move mountains. If Jesus does not give it you, you do not have it. Mountain-moving faith comes from nowhere else but Jesus Christ. The Bible says, *"Looking unto Jesus the author and finisher of our faith; who for the joy that was set before him endured the cross, despising the shame, and is set down at the right hand of the throne of God."*[3] Our faith starts with Jesus and is also completed by Him. Jesus is the only supplier of mountain-moving faith; you can receive it from nowhere else.

Positive thinking must never be mistaken for divine faith. Positive thinking can look similar to faith, but it is not the real thing. Many have shamed the gospel by trying to replace positive thinking for faith. Thinking positive is not a bad thing, but it is surely not the same thing as faith. Positive thinking can never move mountains; only faith that comes from Jesus Christ can do that.

The Bible tells us that *God has given us each a measure of faith.*[4] God has given each of us the faith we need to live the life He has called us to live. If we try to do something that is out of God's will, it is not going to be successful because God has not given us that measure of faith. Mountain-moving faith is measured out and given to each of us as needed.

Faith that works, moves mountains, and heals the sick—the kind of faith that is full of the power of Heaven to accomplish God's will on earth—comes only from Jesus Christ. This faith is full of God's power and must be given by Jesus; no man can take it, and no man can fake it.

The apostle Paul said that he was living as a born-again man, doing what he was called to do by the faith of Jesus Christ. It was not faith or belief in Christ; it was "by the faith of" Christ. Listen to what he says, *"I am crucified with Christ: nevertheless I live; yet not I, but Christ liveth in me: and the life* *which I now live in the flesh I live **by the faith of the Son of God**, who loved me, and gave himself for me.*"⁵ The faith did not belong to Paul but to Jesus. Jesus gave Paul the faith to do what God wanted him to do; Jesus does the same for us today.

On one particular occasion Jesus was speaking to His disciples about forgiveness. Jesus told them if their brother were to sin against them seven times in one day, and each time go to them and ask them to forgive him, they were to do it. This had to seem like an impossible task, to forgive someone who had sinned against them seven times in one day. The apostles knew they could not do it on their own. They did not have the faith required to accomplish such a task. The apostles turned to the only one who could supply them with the faith they would need to do what Jesus told them to do. They turned to Jesus and said, *"Lord, increase our faith."*⁶ Jesus was the source of their faith. To forgive someone seven times in one day is a mountain of a task; and as such, it requires mountain-moving faith. Jesus is the only supplier of mountain-moving faith. This kind of faith comes from no other source.

In the book of Acts we read of a woman named Tabitha who was a follower of Jesus Christ. Tabitha lived in a town called Joppa. Tabitha did a lot of good works for God's Kingdom. One day Tabitha died. The other disciples in Joppa heard that Peter was in a nearby town, so they went and got him. They brought Peter to Tabitha in hopes that he would bring her back to life. When Peter entered the room where Tabitha's body lay, he put everyone else outside. When all were outside, he knelt down and prayed. After he prayed he turned to the body and said, "Tabitha, arise".[7] When he said this, Tabitha sat up in the bed; the breath of life was once again in her body.

Before Peter could tell the dead to rise, he had to go to the Lord to receive the "faith" it would take to raise Tabitha up. The kind of faith that raises the dead can come from no other source than Jesus Christ. Peter did not doubt the power of God to raise the dead, but he had to seek the Lord's will concerning this matter. Peter had a request; but before he could tell the dead to rise, he had to receive a "Yes" from the Lord.

Again in the book of Acts, we read of a time when Peter and John were on their way to the temple. When they came to the temple gate, they came across a beggar who was crippled from birth, unable to walk. Daily the crippled beggar was carried to the temple gates to ask people for money. When the beggar saw Peter and John, he asked them for money. Peter looked at the man and told him that they had no silver or gold, but they did have something to give. Peter took the man by his hand and said, "In the name of Jesus Christ of Nazareth, walk."[8] The man immediately received strength in his legs and stood up. He ran into the temple celebrating. When the people saw it, they thought that perhaps Peter and John had done this on their own. Peter let them know that this man was healed only through Jesus Christ. Peter said, *"By faith in the name of Jesus, this man whom you see and know was made strong. It is Jesus' name and the faith that comes through him that has given this complete healing to him, as you can all see."*[9] The faith needed to heal this man could come from only one source, Jesus Christ. Faith that heals and that moves the mountains we face in this life comes only from Jesus. No matter how much Peter wanted to, he could never have told the man to rise up if he had not first received the faith to do so from Jesus Christ.

FAITH CALLS THINGS
THAT ARE NOT AS THOUGH THEY WERE

We read in the Bible of a man named Abraham. Abraham desperately wanted a child of his own, but he was very old and was fearful he would die childless. Everything around Abraham must have told him that he would not have a child with his wife Sarah— everything except God. God told Abraham he would one day be a great nation, and he would have a child with Sarah. Despite Abraham's age or the age of his wife, and regardless of what anyone told him, when God said, "yes" to Abraham's request to have a child, Abraham received the faith he needed to have that child. It was at this point Abraham could confess he would one day be a great nation, even though at the time he had no child with Sarah. Faith that comes from the Lord confesses God's Word regardless of what is seen. Faith lives and walks by the Word of God, not by what is seen.

*(As it is written, I have made thee a father of many nations,) before him whom he believed, even God, who quickeneth the dead, and **calleth those things which be not as though they were.** Who against hope believed in hope, that he might become the father of many nations, according to that which was spoken, So shall thy seed be.*

And being not weak in faith, he considered not his own body now dead, when he was about an hundred years old, neither yet the deadness of Sara's womb: He staggered not at the promise of God through unbelief; but was strong in faith, giving glory to God And being fully persuaded that, what he had promised, he was able also to perform.[10]

God calls those things that have not yet come to pass as though they had already happened. When we receive God's Word, we may do the same. We cannot force God to do something by merely confessing it; but when God tells us that it will come to pass, faith counts it done. The Bible teaches us, *"Faith comes by hearing, and hearing by the word of God."*[11] Faith hears God's promise—His Word—and trusts Him no matter how crazy or impossible it may seem. We are assured that God's Word will never return empty; it will always do what it was sent out to do.[12]

In the Bible we read of a time when the apostle Paul was headed to Rome by ship. The weather took a turn for the worse. The weather became so bad that everyone on board thought they all were going to die; everybody, that is, except Paul. Paul had received a Word from God that no one aboard would die. In the storm this had to sound like a crazy statement. The wind, the waves, the rain—all told a different story. Some, if not all, the ship's passengers would surely die. Yet, despite the ever so real circumstances the passengers faced, Paul could stand and confess that no one aboard would die. Paul could only make this confession because he had received a Word directly from God, not from any man. Paul said, *"Wherefore, sirs, be of good cheer: for I believe God, that it shall be even as it was told me."*[13]

When we receive a Word from God, it is then that we can confess and stand on it; for no matter how long it takes, the Word God has spoken into our lives will come to pass.

TRUE FAITH ACTS ON GOD'S WORD

"By faith Noah, being warned of God of things not seen as yet, moved with fear, prepared an ark to the saving of his house; by the which he condemned the world, and became heir of the righteousness which is by faith."[14]

Noah was asked by God to do a very strange thing, to build a boat. Not just any boat, but an ark

49

bigger than a football field. For one hundred twenty years Noah worked to build this ark. He must have received incredible ridicule for toiling all that time on what had to seem a worthless task. But Noah had received a Word from God, and he acted on it. Noah was a human man, and this Word from God had to baffle his mind; yet despite this, he still did what God said. Noah trusted and believed God. Noah acted with divine faith that he received from God by His divine Word. He built the ark, saving mankind.

James writes *"be ye doers of the word, and not hearers only"* and that *"faith without works is dead."*[15] Faith that comes from God moves us to action, and it never fails regardless of the circumstances. Faith that is only positive thinking goes nowhere, and in the face of adversity will always crumble and fail.

The book of Hebrews says, *"By faith Abraham, when he was called to go out into a place which he should after receive for an inheritance, obeyed; and he went out, not knowing whither he went."*[16] God told Abraham to leave his home country and that He would bless him and make him a great nation. Abraham received the Word of God and acted on it. Abraham was called and he went. Abraham did not decide to leave on his own; he had a direct Word from God. God imparted faith to Abraham, and it was God who told him to leave. If I am trying to do something that God has not told me to do, it is not by the faith of God no matter how good it may seem.

It is only the faith of God that can move mountains, so it is only when God calls me to move the mountain that I have the faith to do so. If I try to do it of my own will and determination, it is not faith. It may be positive thinking, but that is not the same as divine faith that comes from the Lord. Once God calls me to move a mountain and His faith is imparted to me, it is up to me to put that faith into action and be obedient to His word.

[1] Hebrews 11:1
[2] Luke 5:12-13
[3] Hebrews 12:2
[4] Romans 12:3
[5] Galatians 2:20
[6] Luke 17:5
[7] Acts 9:40
[8] Acts 3:1-6
[9] Acts 3:16 (N.I.V.)
[10] Romans 4:17-21
[11] Romans 10:17
[12] Isaiah 55:11
[13] Acts 27:25
[14] Hebrews 11:7
[15] James 1:22
[16] Hebrews 11:8

Chapter Seven

RECEIVING YOUR ANSWERED PRAYER

"If ye then, being evil, know how to give good gifts unto your children, how much more shall your Father which is in heaven give good things to them that ask him?"
Matthew 7:11

God wants to give His children good things. God wants to answer our prayers whether the answer is "Yes" or "No." Perhaps there have been times when you knew God's will, prayed for it, yet never saw it come to pass. The problem does not lie with God's ability or desire to answer our prayers. I believe many times our prayers go unanswered because we do not know how to receive. We must know how to receive what God has for us. At first glance this may seem like the easy part of prayer; we are always ready to receive. Even though Christians are willing to receive from God, often they miss out because they don't know how to receive. In this chapter we will speak about how to receive your answered prayer.

TO RECEIVE WE SHOULD NOT LIMIT GOD

Many times we do not receive our request from the Lord because we limit Him. We limit God with our own imaginations. We look for a way God could perform our request; and when we can't figure it out, we assume it is not possible. Just because we cannot figure out the "how" and "why" behind something does not mean it is impossible for God. Jesus said, *"If thou canst believe, all things are possible to him that believeth."*[1] Many times I believe God wants to answer our request, but we have put OUR limitations on Him. The Bible is clear; with God **nothing is impossible**.[2] If we want to receive the answer to our prayers, we must stop putting limits on God, stop trying to figure Him out.

In Chapter Four we spoke of a time in the Bible after God had taken the children of Israel out of Egypt and was about to bring them into the land of Canaan, the land which He had promised to give to them. Moses sent twelve men to spy out the land. When the spies returned, they described what a bountiful land it truly was. The land was all they had hoped for and more! There was one problem though; giants occupied the land. All but two of the spies proclaimed that they were as grasshoppers compared to the people of the land; and even though it was a bountiful land, there was no way they could possess it as God had promised. The people believed the negative report of the spies about the land; the people took the word of man over the Word of God. Because they did not believe God could deliver the land to them as He had promised, they did not receive it. The Bible says, *"Yea, they turned back and tempted God, and limited the Holy One of Israel."*[3]

The people put limitations on God. They looked at the giants of the land and could not figure out how God could bring them into a land occupied by people of such incredible physical stature. The children of Israel put their limits on a limitless God. Because of this, the people would not enter into the land God had promised them. They would roam the desert for forty years, and the promise would be received by their children—all because they put limits on God. When we put our limits on God, we miss out on what God has for us, not because God does not want us to have it, but because we just can't believe the God of all the Universe is without limits. Nothing is too hard for God!

TO RECEIVE
WE SHOULD NOT PUT GOD IN A BOX

Many times we do not receive our prayer requests because we try to put God in a box. We make a request to the Lord, and then we tell Him how He should do it. I believe God tries to give us the desires of our hearts, but He often does it in a way that we are not expecting or looking for. Because we have a preconceived notion of how God should answer our prayers, we many times overlook God's answer.

The Bible tells us that God's way of doing things is not always the same as we think it should be done. *"For my thoughts are not your thoughts, neither are your ways my ways, saith the LORD. For as the heavens are higher than the earth, so are my ways higher than your ways, and my thoughts than your thoughts."*[4] God sees a picture we do not, and He has His own reason for doing things like He does. If we want to receive our prayer request from the Lord, we must allow Him to do it His way and not try to put Him in a box of our own design.

In the Bible we read of a man named Naaman. Naaman was the captain of the Syrian army. He was a man of great power, but he had the skin disease of leprosy. Naaman heard of a mighty prophet in the land of Israel named Elisha. He sought out Elisha, believing that by the power of God this prophet could and would heal him. When Naaman came to Elisha's house, the prophet did not come out to speak with him. He simply gave his servant instructions to tell Naaman to go and dip himself in the Jordan River seven times, and his skin disease would clear up. Naaman was very angry; he had expected the man of God to come out to him and call on the name of the Lord, striking his hands over his skin, and in doing this he would recover.[5]

Naaman had a preconceived idea about how God was going to answer his request. Even though

God gave him the answer he wanted, it did not come in the package he was expecting. Naaman almost missed out on his answer because he tried to put God in a box. Naaman's servant talked him into doing what the prophet had instructed him to do; and when he did, his skin disease was cured. Naaman did it God's way and received his request.

I have heard a joke told several times that really helps to illustrate how God answers our prayers. There was once a man living a home that was in a dangerous flood zone. As the rains continued to come and all the surrounding homes were evacuated, the man decided to stay and pray to the Lord to deliver him. Shortly after the man finished praying, a fire truck pulled up outside looking for anyone who might have been left behind; but the man refused to go in the fire truck because he had prayed to God and believed that God would deliver him. As the waters continued to rise, the inside of the man's home was flooded; so he climbed up on top of the roof. While he was on the roof, some people in a boat passed by and tried to get him to come with them. The man held to the hope that God would still deliver him. The water continued to rise and eventually came up to the man's neck. At that very moment a helicopter flew overhead and a ladder was thrown down for the man to grab; but he refused, saying he was trusting in God. Soon after, the waters overtook the man and he died. When the Lord met him at the gates of Heaven, the man was understandably upset and expressed his disappointment to the Lord. He had prayed for deliverance, trusted God, and waited for Him; but his prayer was never answered. The Lord asked the man, "Why are you upset? We sent you a fire truck, a boat, and a helicopter!" The man's prayer was answered, but it came in a package that did not meet his preconceived notion of how God would provide for him. This man is like many Christians today, wanting God to answer their prayers, but wanting Him to do it their way. Allow God to be God!

You cannot put God in a box. He will not stay there. God does things His own way. When Jesus walked this earth, He went about healing people; but he did it in many different ways. At times Jesus merely spoke to them; other times he touched them. Then there were times He did seemingly strange things—like spitting on the ground, making mud and rubbing it on a blind man's eyes, and giving him instructions to wash his eyes in a certain pool of water. When the man did as Jesus said, his sight returned.[6]

Allow God to answer your prayer the way He wants; after all, He is God! Don't miss your answer because it does not come the way you think it should. Just because the gift does not come in the wrapping paper you expected does not mean you didn't get the gift you wanted.

TO RECEIVE WE SHOULD NOT TEMPT GOD

We read in the Bible about when Jesus was baptized and the Holy Spirit descended on Him; and how afterwards, the Spirit led Him out into the wilderness. Jesus was in the wilderness for forty days being tempted by the devil. After forty days Jesus was hungry, and the devil tried to tempt Him in several ways. At one point the devil took Jesus up to the pinnacle of the temple. He told Jesus that if He was really the Son of God to cast himself down because God would send His angels to save Him. Satan quoted scripture, using it out of context and out of line with the rest of God's Word; he tried to mislead Jesus. Jesus replied, *"It is said, Thou shalt not tempt the Lord thy God."*[7]

In the Book of Psalms it is written that God will give His angels charge over us; however, to jump off a building and tempt God is not only crazy, it is unscriptual. As crazy as it may seem to tempt God, as Christians we do it all the time. We pray for something and then act contrary to our prayers. Take, for example, the man who is having heart and high blood pressure problems yet refuses to exercise and eat correctly. Another example might be someone who is praying for a job, but never gets off the couch to go look for one. Or consider the person who is praying for peace in the family, but refuses to talk to them.

God is not a genie in a magic lamp, and we should not treat Him that way. If we are praying for a job, we need to get up and look for one. The Bible teaches us, *"Be not deceived; God is not mocked: for whatsoever a man soweth, that shall he also reap."*[8]

We must get up and allow the faith of Jesus Christ inside us to move and work. Faith that is real works, and it does not tempt God. If we want our prayers to be answered, we must not tempt God. God is not under our command; He is the Creator of the entire universe and should be treated with respect and love, not like a genie in a magic lamp. God is clearly our provider; and whatever we receive, it is from Him. He gives us our request because He loves us, not because He is forced at our command. If you want your prayers to be answered, don't tempt God; move on what you have requested from God and trust Him to fulfill your request. Always remember, *"Except the LORD build the house, they labour in vain that build it: except the LORD keep the city, the watchman waketh but in vain."* [ix]

TO RECEIVE WE SHOULD RELY ON GRACE

We ask through Jesus; we must receive through Jesus. We receive our prayer request based on what Jesus has done, not on what we have done. In the Book of Acts, we read of a time after the resurrection and ascension of Jesus Christ that a disciple named Philip went down to a city in Samaria. While in the city, Philip preached the Gospel and worked many signs and wonders. Because of all the wonders he did, the people believed on Jesus Christ. Among those who believed on Jesus was a certain man named Simon. The Bible teaches us that Simon was a sorcerer and had astonished the Samaritan people with his acts of sorcery. Simon was baptized by Philip and went around with Philip as he worked many miracles in Samaria. When the apostles in Jerusalem heard that the Samaritans had received the Gospel, they sent Peter and John to them. Peter and John, putting their hands on the believers, prayed for them that they would receive the Holy Spirit, and they did. When Simon saw that the Holy Spirit was given to those on whom the apostles laid their hands, he offered them money if they would give him the ability to do the same to whomever he laid his hands on. Peter said to him, *"Thy money perish with thee, because thou hast thought that the gift of God may be purchased with money. Thou hast neither part nor lot in this matter: for thy heart is not right in the sight of God."*[10]

Simon wanted the gift of God and sought to purchase it with money. Simon's heart was not right with God. He had not grasped the concept of grace. He never understood that grace was what would make him right with God. Simon foolishly thought he could buy what he wanted from God. God is not in the retail business; He is not out on the corner trying to sell us blessings. As ridiculous as it may seem for Simon to try to buy what he wanted from God, I have found many times Christians unwittingly do the same thing today. Instead of using money to try to buy the gifts and blessings of God, they use their good deeds. They think if they can just do enough good deeds and stay away from sin, then God will surely grant their prayer request. Like Simon, they have not grasped the concept that God's gifts are to be received, not earned. The Bible says, *"For by grace are ye saved through faith; and that not of yourselves: it is the gift of God: Not of works, lest any man should boast."*[11]

We receive the gift of salvation by grace; we simply trust in Christ. Everything we receive from our Father in Heaven is by grace. We cannot earn merit for ourselves before God, but we continually try. I have found God blessing me the most when I have messed up the most. It is at these times I knew I deserved nothing from God, and yet this is when I have received the most. On the other hand, there have been times when I have really done well; I have stayed away from sin, done all the things the Bible instructs, and then wondered why God was not answering my prayers. I could not understand; I was doing everything I should do, and still my prayers were not answered. One day God revealed to me that I, like Simon, was trying to buy His gifts and blessings. I thought if I really did "good" and kept God's rules, He would surely give me the request of my lips and the desires of my heart.

God showed me that there was nothing I could do to earn my prayer request; I could only receive it.

Many times as Christians we rely on our own works, and not the works of Jesus Christ. The truth is no matter how "good" we are, we are never "good" enough to receive what God has. We try so hard to earn God's favor; we think if we can just continue to do the right things, God will surely grant our requests. The truth is no matter how hard we try, we will never be good enough to earn God's blessings. The only one who ever walked this earth that did that "good" was Jesus Christ; and it is only by depending on His finished work, trusting in Him and not our own works, that we will ever receive anything from God. We ask through Jesus; we must also receive through Jesus. Too often we ask through Jesus and try to receive through ourselves.

TO RECEIVE WE SHOULD UNDERSTAND
OUR RELATIONSHIP WITH GOD

Our relationship with God is based totally on what Jesus has done and has nothing to do with our works. We make the choice to receive Jesus and trust in Him for our salvation, but He has done all the work. This is a fact that most are aware of when we first receive Jesus Christ as our Lord and Savior; but as we continue in our Christian lives, we sometimes forget and start to rely on our own works to keep us right with God. We must understand that no matter how long we are Christians, our relationship with God will and must always rely on the finished work of Jesus

Christ. We understand that the work was indeed finished by Jesus on the cross, and there is nothing we can add to it. The Bible says, *"Therefore by the deeds of the law there shall no flesh be justified in his sight: for by the law is the knowledge of sin."*[12] The Laws of God, His rules and regulations, do not make people right, they only show us right from wrong; it is only Jesus that makes people right in God's sight. When we call on God and try to justify ourselves before Him, we will always fall short; and if we are trying to justify ourselves, we will never have our prayer requests answered. Again, the Bible says this: *"Being justified freely by his grace through the redemption that is in Christ Jesus:"*[13]. We are freely justified by what Jesus has done. All we have to do is receive it.

We have been set free from the duty of self-justification. Self-justification depends on our own works to make us right with God. Grace depends only on Jesus; Jesus is the gift of God's grace! The Bible says, *"For God so loved the world, that he gave his only begotten Son, that whosoever believeth in him should not perish, but have everlasting life."*[14] Jesus is literally God's grace embodied. Again the Bible says, *"For the law was given by Moses, but grace and truth came by Jesus Christ."*[15] Jesus is God's free gift of grace that no man or woman is worthy of; but because of God's great love for us, He poured out His grace in the form of Jesus Christ for all who are willing to receive it.

We must understand that our relationship with God is based totally on what Jesus has done; we are made right with God only through Christ. *"For he hath made him to be sin for us, who knew no sin; that we might be made the righteousness of God in him."*[16] We are only right with God through Jesus. No matter how hard we try, we can never earn God's favor, goodness, or mercy; we can only receive it through Jesus Christ. Our Father in Heaven answers our prayers because of what Jesus has done by bringing us into a right relationship with God through Himself.

The Bible tells of a time when God was getting ready to bring the nation of Israel into the land He had promised to their fathers. Israel had just finished roaming the wilderness for forty years for tempting God and not trusting Him. Now God was ready to fulfill the Word He had spoken to their fathers. God reminds them that he is giving them this land, not based on their righteousness, but because of the wickedness of the people who were currently in the land and because of the promise He had made to their fathers.[17] Likewise, God answers our prayers not because of our righteousness but because of what Jesus Christ has done—because of His righteousness. We must always depend on the work of Jesus to make and keep us right with God. Our relationship with the Father is based on our relationship with His only-begotten Son, Jesus Christ. Our Father in Heaven hears our prayers when we call and answers them because of our right standing with Him through Jesus

Christ. Our prayers will not be answered if we do not understand that we are made right with God because of what Jesus has done, and it has nothing to do with our own works. No matter how "good" we think we are, or how well we seem to be doing, it is never "good" enough to make us right with God. It truly is all about Jesus when it comes to our relationship with God!

TO RECEIVE
WE SHOULD EXPECT AN ANSWER

"My voice shalt thou hear in the morning, O LORD; in the morning will I direct my prayer unto thee, and will look up."[18] The psalmist said he would direct his prayers to the God in Heaven, and then he would look up. The psalmist is looking up to Heaven because he expects an answer. When we make a request, it seems logical to expect an answer; yet many Christians don't. They are conditioned to pray when needed, but are never looking for God to respond. They simply pray as they've been taught and go back about their business, never looking for or even expecting God to respond to their cry. This is a mistake!

When we pray, we must expect an answer. If we are not looking for an answer to our prayer, why pray? It is a waste of time to pray if we do not expect God to answer us when we call on Him. When we pray we must understand that we have just called on the Almighty, the Creator of all things, and we should expect an answer. Whether the answer to our prayer request is "yes" or "no" we must look for—and expect—an answer from the Lord.

In Chapter Five we spoke of the prophet Elijah. Elijah lived during the reign of king Ahab of Israel. During Ahab's reign God closed up the skies, and it did not rain for three years. During this time the Bible says there was a great famine in the city of Samaria. God told Elijah that it was going to rain. Elijah declared to Ahab that rain was coming. Elijah had the seed of God's Word, and he acted on it. Even though Elijah knew God's will and had declared it to the king, Elijah still prayed for the rain to come. The prophet went to the top of Mount Carmel, bent down, and put his face between his knees. Elijah was praying for God's will to come to pass on the earth. Elijah prayed and then sent his servant to go and look out toward the sea for rain. His servant returned with word that he saw no sign of rain. Elijah sent his servant back a second time, and he returned with the same report—no sign of rain. Elijah did not quit looking. He had God's Word concerning the matter and he prayed for it; now he expected an answer. Elijah sent his servant back seven times looking for an answer to his prayer, and on the seventh time his servant returned with a report that he saw a cloud rise out of the sea; rain was on its way.[19]

Elijah expected an answer, and he continued to look until he got one. Elijah did not see his prayer request granted after the first time, but he did not give up on God. Just because God said it would happen did not mean it was going to happen right away. Elijah never gave up. He expected an answer and continued to look until he received it. When we pray, we must expect an answer. We must pray and look up for God's response. If we are not looking and expecting God to respond to our call, we should not be surprised when He doesn't respond.

The Bible also records the story of a woman who had an uncontrollable bleeding problem. The woman's problem had persisted for twelve years. She had tried to get help for her issue of blood but was unable to find anyone able to help her. One day Jesus was passing through the town she resided in, and many people went out to greet Him. The crowd was pushed against Jesus to the point they almost crushed Him; everyone wanted to see Him and be close to Him. The woman knew this was her chance. No one else had been able to heal her; but if she could just get close enough to touch Jesus, she knew without a doubt she would be healed. The woman made her way through the crowd; reaching out, she touched the edge of his cloak and immediately her bleeding stopped.[20]

Jesus stopped. He knew something had happened. He had felt power go out from Him when the woman touched him. Jesus asked who had touched Him. His disciples had to be puzzled because so many people were pressed against Him; Peter said to Him, "Everyone is crowding around you." There were probably hundreds of people touching Jesus and trying to get to Him; but there was only one who was expecting to get something from Him once she got to Him, and that was the woman with the uncontrollable bleeding problem. She was going to Jesus with a need, and she was expecting to get something when she got to Him; and she did! When we call on the Lord, we cannot be content just knowing our prayers reach Him through Jesus; we must expect to receive an answer back through Jesus. If we are not looking and expecting an answer to our prayers, like the woman with the bleeding problem did, there is a good chance we will miss out on God's provision. When we pray, we must expect an answer; we must look for an answer and not give up looking, no matter how long it takes!

TO RECEIVE WE SHOULD
LOOK TO THE GIVER OF ALL GOOD THINGS

"I will lift up mine eyes unto the hills, from whence cometh my help. My help cometh from the LORD, which made heaven and earth."[21] If we want to receive from the Lord, we should look to Him. I need to lift my eyes off my problems and struggles and stay focused on the One who is able to answer my call for help. The apostle Paul said it this way: *"Finally, brethren, whatsoever things are true, whatsoever things are honest, whatsoever things are just, whatsoever things are pure, whatsoever things are lovely, whatsoever things are of good report; if there be any virtue, and if there be any praise, think on these*

things."[22] To stay focused on the Lord is to think on *"these things."* When I am thinking on *"these things,"* my mind and eyes are off my struggles and on the One who can do something about them.

This is one reason why praising God is so important. When I am praising God, I am making a choice to look on the *"Giver of all good things,"* the Lord. My answered prayer is going to come from nowhere else, so I should look nowhere else when I am looking to receive from God. I must look to the Lord. Praise is an all-day, all-activity thing. Whether I am praising God directly or indirectly, with words or by the way I live my life, praise should continually be part of my life. Praising God is not a one-hour activity performed on Sunday morning; praise is a way of life that is constantly focused on God, the *"Giver of all good things."* If I am not praising God, my eyes and attention will most likely be somewhere else; and if I am not looking to the Lord, I may very well miss what He is trying to give me. Praise keeps my eyes on the One holding the answer to my prayer.

When God led the children of Israel out of Egypt, they would end up spending forty years in the desert. As Israel traveled through the desert, headed to the land of promise God had sworn to give to their fathers, the tribe of Judah led the way. Israel was made up of twelve tribes. They would camp in the desert wherever God told them to stop; and when God was ready to move, they would pack up and leave. God instructed Moses that the tribe of Judah would be the first tribe to leave each time. The tribe of Judah would lead the nation of Israel through the desert following God to the land of promise.[23]

As we discussed in Chapter Four, the word Judah literally means "praise." "Praise" was leading Israel toward God and the promise He had made to their fathers. "Praise" would guide the nation to the Promised Land. Praise will lead us to God and keep us focused on God who holds the answer to our prayers. We may miss out on receiving simply because we are not in the same place as the "Giver of all good things." Praise will lead us to the Lord, who is the only one able to answer our prayers. Praise keeps us focused on the Lord, following His lead to our promised land.

In the New Testament book of Acts, we read of Paul and Silas. While they were ministering in the town of Thyatira, they were beaten and thrown into prison. They had real problems, but they knew exactly what to do in their time of distress and persecution; they called on the Lord! Paul and Silas prayed, they made their request to the Lord, and then they began to sing songs of praise. As they were singing, there was a great earthquake; the whole prison shook. All the doors of the prison were opened, and everyone's chains came loose.[24] Wow!

Paul and Silas did not pray and then turn around and focus on their problem of being beaten and thrown into prison; they did not sulk or complain. They made a choice—a conscious decision to sing praises to the "Giver of all good things," the Lord. Praise led them to the One holding their answered prayer. Praise takes our eyes off our problems, which we tend to focus on, and puts them on Christ. Our eyes and attention should be focused on the solution, not the problem! Praise will lead you to the Lord, the only place you will be able to receive the answer to your prayer.

[1] Mark 9:23
[2] Luke 1:37
[3] Psalms 78:41
[4] Isaiah 55:8-9
[5] 2 kings 5:10-11
[6] John 9:1-7
[7] Luke 4:12
[8] Galatians 6:7
[9] Psalm 127:1
[10] Acts 8:9-21
[11] Ephesians 2:8-9
[12] Romans 3:20
[13] Romans 3:24
[14] John 3:16
[15] John 1:17
[16] 2 Corinthians 5:21
[17] Deuteronomy 9:1-6
[18] Psalm 5:3
[19] 1 Kings chapter 18
[20] Luke 8:44-45
[21] Psalm 121:1-2
[22] Philippians 4:8
[23] Numbers 2:9
[24] Acts 16:25-26

Chapter Eight

FASTING

"And Jesus said unto them, Can the children of the bridechamber mourn, as long as the bridegroom is with them? but the days will come, when the bridegroom shall be taken from them, and then shall they fast."
Matthew 9:15

The act of fasting is found throughout the Bible, both Old and New Testaments. Fasting shows up throughout the Bible when ordinary people like you and I need the amazing power and provision of an extraordinary God to overcome seemingly impossible circumstances. Fasting is intermingled with prayer in the scriptures. It appears as a "battering ram" in our prayer life that moves us to focus on God, the *"giver of all good things."* Fasting is the "nitric oxide" boost in our prayer lives.

There are three main types of fasts found throughout the scriptures. One is a fast from food and water. The second is a fast from just food. These two fasts are commonly found in the Bible. A third fast, not so common, is found in the Book of Daniel where Daniel eats no meat, pleasant bread, or wine.[1] He seems to abstain from things pleasing to the taste buds, things we may desire beyond their nutritional value. We also find supernatural fasting such as Moses did. While in the presence of God, Moses went forty days without eating or drinking.[2]

When I fast, my flesh becomes weak; and when I become weak, God becomes strong. In fact, the Bible teaches that it is in our weakness that God's strength is made perfect in our lives.[3] We depend greatly on our flesh, our own strength and ability. When I fast, it exposes the weakness of my flesh. It is at this point I turn my attention from my own ability, which is exposed as inability, and turn it to God—the only One who is truly capable of anything. Fasting is not a magical formula that forces God to act; it is an act of inward humility demonstrated in the outward act of fasting. Fasting is for my benefit, not God's. In fasting I am able to see that my prayer life can only be fruitful through Christ and that it has nothing to do with my strengths or abilities. Fasting, much like praise, takes my eyes off my "so called" strengths and abilities, which are nothing more than an allusion, and puts them on the One who makes all things possible when I pray.[4]

Fasting is a biblical principle. We are taught in the Bible to turn to God with fasting.[5] Even though we may not fully understand how fasting affects our prayer lives, we trust in God's Word that it does make a difference; we do not lean on our own understanding.[6] When Jesus spoke about how to pray and fast, He did not say *"if"* you fast, but *"when"* you fast. Just as it would be absurd for a Christian not to pray, it is the same for one not to fast. Jesus said regarding fasting, *"Moreover when ye fast, be not, as the hypocrites, of a sad countenance: for they disfigure their faces, that they may appear unto men to fast. Verily I say unto you, They have their reward. But thou, when thou fastest, anoint thine head, and wash thy face; That thou appear not unto men to fast, but unto thy Father which is in secret: and thy Father, which seeth in secret, shall reward thee openly."*[7]

Fasting, like everything else we do, should be done under the guidance of the Holy Spirit. If you have never fasted, I would encourage you to start off small, perhaps a half-day fast, and move on from there. Whatever kind of fast you do, allow the Spirit to guide you in it; and keep in mind that fasting is a biblical principle that goes hand in hand with prayer.

[1] Daniel 10:3
[2] Exodus 34:28
[3] 2 Corinthians 12:9
[4] Philippians 4:13
[5] Joel 2:12
[6] Proverbs 3:5
[7] Matthew 6:16-18

Chapter Nine

WAITING ON GOD

"Be patient therefore, brethren, unto the coming of the Lord. Behold, the husbandman waiteth for the precious fruit of the earth, and hath long patience for it, until he receive the early and latter rain."
James 5:7

It can be frustrating when you are trying to call people, and you can't get them. It is especially frustrating when you have something important you need to speak with them about. Sometime we may have this same experience with God. We are trying to get hold of Him through prayer, but we're not getting a response. We are abiding in Christ, going through Him to get to the Father; we know we have received God's Word and are praying accordingly, but still no answer. It can be very frustrating! David must have experienced this frustration when he wrote, *"How long wilt thou forget me, O LORD? for ever? how long wilt thou hide thy face from me?"* [1] Perhaps you have felt the same way as David, wondering if God has heard your prayer; and if He has, is He ever going to answer. If so, be ENCOURAGED and KNOW!

JUST BECAUSE IT HAS NOT
HAPPENED DOESN'T MEAN IT WILL NOT

If your prayer has not been answered, don't give up hope. Continue to stand on the Word of God. Daniel of the Bible was a mighty man of God. We read of a time when Daniel called on the Lord, but he got no response from God. For twenty days this mighty man of God sought the Lord, but no answer came. Daniel had to feel like David when David said *"how long will thou forget me,"* but God had not forgotten Daniel at all. Daniel did not give up seeking and looking for an answer to his prayer; and on the 21st day after he prayed, he received his answer.

The angel who delivered the answer to Daniel's prayer told him that he was heard when he first called on God and that the answer to his prayer was given; yet, Daniel did not receive it for three weeks. The angel told Daniel the prince of Persia tried to prevent him from getting to Daniel. The prince of Persia was a demonic force fighting to keep Daniel from receiving his answer. The angel tells Daniel that he had to call on Michael, the archangel, to help him, and with his help he was able to make it to Daniel.[2]

Daniel never gave up on God; he made a choice to wait on God and to *keep on keeping on* until his answer came. Daniel's answer was delayed by demonic forces that did not want his prayer answered. Perhaps the same is true for you. You have called on the Lord, but have not received an answer. You wonder if God has even heard you, not realizing your prayer was heard when you first called. The answer was sent; it just hasn't yet made it to you. Don't give up! Maybe there is an angel fighting his way to you right now.

We also read of Habakkuk who witnessed great evil being done in his homeland. He cried out to God about the evil he witnessed, but he got no answer. He wondered why God would not do anything about it, why his prayers were going unanswered. Habakkuk said, *"O LORD, how long shall I cry, and thou wilt not hear! even cry out unto thee of violence, and thou wilt not save!"*[3] Was God listening? Of course He was! God was listening, and He had a plan to do something about the wickedness that was going on. Habakkuk's prayer would be answered eventually, but it would be done in God's time and in God's way.

Just because Habakkuk's prayer did not come to pass right away did not mean it wouldn't. God had heard Him and had something in the works; Habakkuk would just have to wait. Always understand that God does things His own way and in His own time. When you call on God in the name of the Lord Jesus Christ, He hears you right away. If your answer does not arrive right away, don't give up; continue to trust in the Lord, looking for your answer.

WAIT ON GOD

"Therefore turn thou to thy God: keep mercy and judgment, and wait on thy God continually." [4] We go to the Lord in prayer, making our requests known to our Father in Heaven. Once we have done all we can, we must wait on the Lord. Stand on God's Word and wait for Him to move.

Most of us struggle with the concept of waiting. We have a "fast food" mentality. We want to pull up to Jesus, place our order, move up to the window of Heaven, and have it handed to us right away. Unfortunately, God does not work in a "fast food" manner. God does things His own way and in His own time; we must learn to trust and wait on the Lord always! We must trust that God will not forsake us. And no matter how long it takes, if we will continue to trust God and look to Him, He will deliver an answer to our prayer requests.

I would like to look at two men of the Bible. One of them waited and trusted God; the other did not. The first man is Saul. Saul was the first king of Israel. During the beginning of Saul's kingship, Israel was living under the rule of the Philistine nation. Israel was gathered together to fight for their freedom from Philistine oppression. Saul waited for the prophet Samuel to come and offer a sacrifice to God before they went out to battle. Samuel was a prophet and a priest, and only the priests were allowed to offer sacrifice to the Lord. When Samuel did not come right away, Saul became impatient; he saw his men leaving and thought he must take immediate action. Saul could not see or understand that even though some of the men with him were becoming frightened and were leaving, God was not. Saul offered the sacrifice himself; he was tired of waiting, so he took action. Saul did not wait on God, and it cost him. Saul would lose his kingdom to another man, a man after God's heart.[5] When we make a choice to move without God, to try to make our prayer request happen when we think it should, we miss out on God's blessings.

The next man acted quite differently when it came to waiting on and trusting God. This man's name was David. David would become the second king of Israel, replacing Saul. God sent the prophet Samuel to anoint David king when he was about fifteen years old. David did not become king until he was thirty, and even then it was not over all of Israel. David would have to wait seven more years before he received all God had promised—to make him king over all of Israel. David had learned to trust and wait on God. David had at least two opportunities to kill Saul and take the kingdom for himself, but he refused to do it. David had received a promise from God, and he was determined to allow God to deliver what was promised to him. How easy it would have been for David to become impatient and take things into his own hands, but he didn't. God delivered what He had promised David, but He did it in His own way and time, not in David's.[6]

We, like David, must learn to wait on God if we want to receive from Him. We must forsake our "fast food" mentality, and allow God to be God! We spoke of Habakkuk earlier, about how he could not understand why God would not act—why He was not answering his prayer right away. Habakkuk finally learns to wait and watch for God to move. Look at what Habakkuk says, *"I will stand upon my watch, and set me upon the tower, and will watch to see what he will say unto me, and what I shall answer when I am reproved."*[7] If we are going to receive our prayers answered from the Lord, we must learn to trust Him; we must wait and watch for God to move.

GOD'S TIMING

"To every thing there is a season, and a time to every purpose under the heaven:"[8] There is an appointed time for our prayers to be answered, but only God knows that time. Unfortunately, our clock and God's clock don't always match up. God does things in His own timing.

In the Bible there is a story of a man named Lazarus; he and his sisters, Martha and Mary, were friends with Jesus. One day Jesus received word from Lazarus's sisters that he was sick; they wanted Jesus to come and heal him. Jesus received the request, but He waited two more days before He left to go to Lazarus' aid. The Bible is clear that Jesus loved Lazarus and his sisters, yet He did not come immediately even though He knew they needed help. When Jesus finally got there, Martha met Him with the news that Lazarus was dead. It must have appeared to Martha and Mary that Jesus was too late, that their request would go unanswered. They did not realize that Jesus was working by His clock and that He wasn't late at all; in fact, He was right on time! Why had Jesus waited so long? Jesus had waited so that God could be glorified. Jesus would not just heal Lazarus; but He would raise him from the grave, bringing glory to God.[ix] Jesus had received their prayer request, and had every intention of answering it, but it would be in His time and in a way that would bring glory to God.

The Bible says, *"But when the fulness of the time was come, God sent forth his Son, made of a woman, made under the law."*[10] The Father did not send the Son until the time was right. It was not a matter of need because ever since Adam first sinned, the world has needed Jesus. It was a matter of timing. God knew the perfect time to send Jesus into this world. When our prayers are not answered right away, we must realize that it is not because God doesn't hear us or that our needs are not legitimate and fully in line with God's will. It may simply be a matter of timing—God's timing to be specific.

In the book of Revelation, the Bible speaks of vials that are held by twenty elders in Heaven. These vials are filled with the prayers of God's people.

These are prayers that were heard and have not been forgotten, but they are yet to be answered; they will be answered when God says the time is right. Perhaps your prayer is one of these that have been heard and is being stored up for the right time.[11]

As we continue to look at Habakkuk's story, we see that God had indeed heard his prayer request. Now we see that God was preparing a great army from the land of the Chaldeans to do His will. God was getting things prepared to answer Habakkuk's prayer request; it would all be done in God's timing. *"For, lo, I raise up the Chaldeans, that bitter and hasty nation, which shall march through the breadth of the land, to possess the dwelling places that are not theirs."*[12] Perhaps God is getting ready to answer your prayer; perhaps He is putting everything and everyone in place, and soon you will see your request answered and God glorified.

WHAT TO DO WHILE YOU ARE WAITING

"By him therefore let us offer the sacrifice of praise to God continually, that is, the fruit of our lips giving thanks to his name."[13] While you are waiting for God to move, praise Him. When it seems as though everything is falling apart in your life and nothing makes sense, praise Him. We should praise God continually, not just for what He has done, but for who He is. He is the One who loved us so much that He would rather die on a cross than have to live

85

without us! Even when we don't understand God, we should still trust and praise Him, knowing He is working in our best interest in His own way. Remember God's ways are not like ours; don't try to figure Him out, just praise Him and trust Him. Remember, praise is for our benefit, not God's. Praise keeps our eyes on the *"Giver of all good things"* while we wait on the Lord.

When all is falling apart and you feel as if you are losing your mind, take the attitude of the psalmist when he wrote, *"But I will hope continually, and will yet praise thee more and more."*[14] In the storm while you are waiting for God to move, keep your eyes on Him by continually praising Him.

In the Bible we read of a time when the disciples of Jesus were out at sea; Jesus had sent them ahead with the intention of meeting up with them. A storm arose; the winds blew and the waves crashed. As the storm raged, the disciples looked out on the water at what they first thought must be a ghost; it turned out to be Jesus. When Peter realized who it was, he asked the Lord to allow him to come out of the boat to meet Him on the water. Jesus told Peter to come to Him on the water. He stepped out of the boat onto a storm-tossed sea. When Peter kept his eyes on Jesus, he was able to walk on the water through the storm. But Peter took his eyes off Jesus and looked on the storm-tossed sea; and when he did, he began to sink. Jesus had to grab him by the hand and pull him up.[15] If we will keep our eyes on Jesus, we will be able to walk through any storm that life might bring; we will be able to wait on the Lord to move in our prayer lives without growing faint-hearted. But if we, like Peter, take our eyes off the Lord for even a moment, we will begin to sink under the storms of life. We will grow faint-hearted and take things into our own hands, trying to make our prayer request happen in our own way and time instead of trusting God and allowing Him to work in His own way and time.

Habakkuk comes to the conclusion that no matter what happens he will praise God. Listen to what he says: *"Although the fig tree shall not blossom, neither shall fruit be in the vines; the labour of the olive shall fail, and the fields shall yield no meat; the flock shall be cut off from the fold, and there shall be no herd in the stalls: Yet I will rejoice in the LORD, I will joy in the God of my salvation."*[16]

Even though you may not understand what God is doing or why He is not answering you right away, know that your prayers have not fallen on deaf ears. Know that God will move, but it will be in His time. While you wait on the Lord to move, praise Him continually. Remember, praise will keep your eyes on the only One able to answer your prayer.

[1] Psalms 13:1
[2] Daniel 10:1-13
[3] Habakkuk 1:2
[4] Hosea 12:6
[5] 1 Samuel 13:8-14
[6] 2 Samuel 5:4-5
[7] Habakkuk 2:1
[8] Ecclesiastes 3:1
[9] John 11:1-44
[10] Galatians 4:4
[11] Revelations 5:8
[12] Habakkuk 1:6
[13] Hebrews 13:5
[14] Psalms 71:14
[15] Matthew 14:23-31
[16] Habakkuk 3:17-18

Chapter Ten

INTERCEDING FOR OTHERS

"I exhort therefore, that, first of all, supplications, prayers, intercessions, and giving of thanks, be made for all men;
For kings, and for all that are in authority; that we may lead a quiet and peaceable life in all godliness and honesty."
1Timothy 2:1-2

When we accept Jesus Christ as our Lord and Savior, we become children of God through Him. As children of God, we are in the army of God. We are called to intercede for others—for our brothers and sisters in Christ, and also for those who do not know Jesus as Lord and Savior. We read of a time when many had gathered to see Jesus. The house where Jesus spoke was so packed that no one other than those who were already in the house could get to Jesus. There was a certain paralytic man who desperately needed to see Jesus, but had no way to get to Him. Because he could not get to Jesus on his own, four of his friends picked up the bed he was on and carried him to Jesus. When they got to the house, it was so packed they could not get through the door. The four friends carried the paralytic man up to the roof and let him down through the ceiling to Jesus. These four knew their friend had to get to Jesus but could not do it on his own, so they stopped at no length to get their friend to Jesus.[1]

There are many out there who need Jesus but they, like the paralytic man, cannot get to Him on their own. They need someone who cares enough to pick them up and carry them to the throne of grace and lay them before Jesus. As children of God in the army of God, that is what we are to do for others. Jesus is at the right hand of the Father interceding for us, and we must intercede for others.[2] Like the four friends of the paralytic man, we must go to any length to carry to Jesus those who have been beaten down by the circumstances of life and can no longer walk to Him and those who do not know the way to Him. We carry these people to Jesus through intense prayer and fasting. The power of God is able to turn their lives around; we just have to get them before the throne of Jesus Christ.

INTERCEDING FOR THE LOST

Jesus said, *"No man can come to me, except the Father which hath sent me draw him: and I will raise him up at the last day."*[3] No man or woman comes to call on Jesus for salvation on his own; he or she must be drawn by the Holy Spirit. Our testimonies will make little difference in the lives of others if the Holy

Spirit does not open their hearts to receive the message of salvation through Jesus Christ. The Spirit must go before us to open the heart's door for our testimony to be received by others. This happens when we pray for the lost. We must lift the lost up in prayer before Christ and allow the Holy Spirit to open their hearts and eyes.

We read of a time in the book of Acts when Paul and Silas were sharing the Word of God with a group of women. Among these women was a merchant named Lydia. Lydia was able to receive their message because the Spirit of God had gone before Paul and Silas and opened her heart.[4] Had the Holy Spirit not prepared her heart for the message, she would not have been able to come to Christ and receive salvation. If the lost are going to be saved, we are going to have to lift them up before Christ and allow the Spirit of God to prepare their hearts for the message of the Gospel we have for them.

INTERCEDE FOR THE SAINTS

The Bible teaches us that we are to pray for our brothers and sisters in Christ: *"Praying always with all prayer and supplication in the Spirit, and watching thereunto with all perseverance and supplication for all saints."* [5] The *"saints"* are the children of God, those who have accepted Jesus as their Lord and Savior. We are to lift one another up in prayer. We are to stand with each other, calling on the Lord together.

We are taught to look after the needs of our brothers and sisters; we must take care of each other.[6]

We read in the Bible of a time when king Herod had Peter arrested and put in jail. Herod had plans to bring him to public trial after the Passover. Peter was in a bad situation, but he would not have to stand alone. The Bible says that the church earnestly prayed for Peter. Peter's brothers and sisters in Christ did not forget about him; they took up his cause with the Lord. Their prayers were heard and answered when God sent an angel to rescue Peter from prison.[7] Like the early church, we must pray for one another and with one another. There is incredible power when the saints of God gather together and earnestly seek the Lord.

INTERCEDE FOR RULERS

When Judah was carried off to Babylon for their rebellion against the Lord, God tells them to pray for the city where He has placed them. Look what God says in the book of Jeremiah: *"And seek the peace of the city whither I have caused you to be carried away captives, and pray unto the LORD for it: for in the peace thereof shall ye have peace."* [8] We must pray for those who are in authority where we live and where we work. Intercessory prayer should be made for them, from our boss at work to the leaders of our country, and for everyone in between. Intercede for them knowing that if things get better for them, things will get better for you where you work and where you live. If you feel they are ungodly, pray even harder for them, knowing your prayer makes a difference.

After Judah had been in captivity for seventy years, God released them. After their release when Darius was king of Persia, instructions were given for the priests to make intercession for the king and his sons.[ix] The priests and leaders were wise to do so for as things got better for the king and his family, things got better for them. As the king saw the glory and goodness of God in and around his life, things became better for the people of God.

INTERCEDE FOR YOUR ENEMIES

Love is the distinguishing earmark of a follower of Christ.[10] It is this love that flows from the Spirit of God living in us that allows us to love and pray, not just for those who love us back, but also for those who oppose us—our enemies. Jesus instructed His followers to love and pray for those who persecuted them. Jesus said, *"But I say unto you, Love your enemies, bless them that curse you, do good to them that hate you, and pray for them which despitefully use you, and persecute you."*[11] Praying for our enemies is not easy to do; but God does expect us to do it, even though it may not feel good.

As the children of God we do not repay evil for evil, but we overcome it with good.[12] When we lift up our enemies before God, we know that if their hearts are changed and they call on the Lord, they will no longer be our enemies. They will become part of our family—the family of God.

As the children of God, we are the army of God on this earth; we must take a stand, picking others up in prayer and carrying them before the Lord. We must kick the gates of Hell back and carry the lost before the throne of Christ. Understand that your prayers are powerful and have the ability to change the world. Always remember *"The effectual fervent prayer of a righteous man availeth much."*[13]

[1] Mark 2:1-2
[2] Romans 8:34
[3] John 6:44
[4] Acts 16:14
[5] Ephesians 6:18
[6] Philippians 2:4
[7] Acts 12:1-10
[8] Jeremiah 29:7
[9] Ezra 6:9-10
[10] John 13:35
[11] Matthew 5:44
[12] Romans 12:21
[13] James 5:16

Additional copies of this book may be
purchased online at
www.powerofprayernow.org

Or

Write to:
Tim Gregory Ministries
5409 Canal Rd.
Santa Fe, TX 77517